2026
ASTROLOGICAL
FORECAST

BY EVA SYLWESTER

Publisher: Eva Sylwester, Eugene, Oregon, United States of America
astrologybooks@proton.me

These horoscopes were originally published on
http://astrologybooks.substack.com in December 2025.

Book design by Eva Sylwester using free Kindlepreneur template.

ISBN (e-book): 979-8-9874394-5-6

ISBN (paperback): 979-8-9874394-6-3

CONTENTS

OVERVIEW

2026 is not likely to be a quiet year, but some of the racket might actually be constructive. We may be capable of looking beyond usual divisions and surface drama to realize that we want a lot of the same things. Money matters could be challenging, but we will at least have a chance to start addressing them in a realistic way.

SATURN AND NEPTUNE

The most significant astrological event of 2026 will be the Saturn-Neptune conjunction. Saturn and Neptune were close to a conjunction for much of 2025 as both passed back and forth over the cusp between Pisces and Aries. However, their one and only exact meeting will take place at 0° Aries on February 20, 2026, shortly after Neptune commits to staying in Aries on January 26 and Saturn does the same on February 13. (Dates given are for the Pacific time zone.)

Saturn craves structure, while Neptune dissolves structure. As Saturn and Neptune have come close to their conjunction in 2025, rhetoric has grown surreal. Popular conspiracy theories involving the Tartarian Empire claim that everything we know about history is a lie, while the nonsensical 6-7 meme commands the attention of the younger generation.

Once the Saturn-Neptune conjunction actually happens at 0° Aries, I expect some of the wild speculation to dissipate. We will have a chance to build a new narrative that makes sense for our current circumstances.

Saturn in Aries could make entrenched power dynamics too visible to ignore. In Weekend Entertainment Guide 8/29/25, I brought up *The Ren & Stimpy Show* as an example of this. It's actually not kind to Stimpy, the character who always gets pushed around, to claim that he's on equal footing with Ren, the character typically doing the pushing. Being totally honest about what *is* going on, even when it's not what *should be* going on, will be necessary before any realistic path forward is possible.

Meanwhile, Neptune speaks to what we collectively idealize at a given time. During the Neptune in Pisces transit, which began in 2011, compassion for the vulnerable was idealized. Although I personally favor some of the changes that took place during this time, such as the legalization of same-sex marriage throughout the United States, I also see how the sentiments of Neptune in Pisces led to the abusive extremes of cancel culture, where no attempt to be good was ever good enough.

With Neptune in individualistic Aries, people might just stop trying to be good. The arts will likely be much improved by the boldness of Aries energy giving artists permission to say what they really think. Daily life, however, might become more challenging as it becomes seen as cool to push past any restriction or boundary just because one can. I still think Stephen Fry unwittingly described the coming Neptune in Aries transit best: "If you want a picture of the future, imagine Veruca Salt stamping her foot and crying, 'I want it now!' — forever."[1]

PLUTO

Transformative Pluto will continue moving through Aquarius, which it first entered in 2023. Already it has shaken up established alliances and increased the role of technology in our daily lives, and these trends are likely to persist.

---

[1] This was in a 2024 Substack post that has since been taken down called "In Touch With The Inner Adult"; I've edited the quote slightly for clarity.

In 2026, revolutionary Uranus will trine Pluto exactly on July 17 and November 29. I am reminded of the Uranus-Pluto square that characterized Barack Obama's presidency, where change happened, but every single step was a great big drama. The Uranus-Pluto trine we are now moving into is a gentler alignment between those two planets, so change is likely to happen in a way that we feel ready for.

Bombastic Jupiter in individualistic Leo will oppose Pluto on July 20, potentially provoking power struggles. The harder some grand Aquarian vision for collective harmony tries to cram everyone into compliance, the more dramatic the pushback is likely to be.

URANUS

Chaotic Uranus began its transit of resource-oriented Taurus in 2018, shaking up our view of money. With rampant inflation, the relationship between effort expended and reward gained often seemed to lose logical coherence. Meanwhile, Bitcoin went from obscure to accessible as people looked for alternatives to a system that they felt unable to get ahead in.

With Uranus settling in Gemini on April 25, 2026, the theatrics around money are likely to settle down, making it clearer what's actually going on. Although cryptocurrency is probably here to stay in some capacity, we may come to see it more realistically — it isn't a savior powerful enough to deliver us from deeper structural problems.

As Uranus transits Gemini, a sign associated with communication, who we consider worthy of talking to might broaden. People we don't fully agree with may still hold insights we find helpful. Although the two-party system that dominates the politics of the United States, a nation founded with Uranus in Gemini, speaks to legitimate and important differences, sometimes the truth is not as simple as one side or the other makes it out to be.

JUPITER

Jupiter will start 2026 in Cancer, where it has been since June 9, 2025. Although Jupiter in Cancer spent much of fall 2025 in a Grand Trine with other placements in Water signs, it will come to be the only outer planet in a Water sign once Saturn and Neptune shift into Aries in early 2026. It will therefore be important to keep track of brewing emotions and address them before they explode.

On June 29, 2026, Jupiter will move into Leo. It will remain there until July 25, 2027. Both Jupiter and Leo, independent of each other, favor grandiose, flamboyant displays. The combination of Jupiter in Leo could therefore be a lot. If we can know when to avoid taking over-the-top statements at face value, it might be mostly fun.

CHIRON

In 2026, Chiron, an asteroid associated with the archetype of the wounded healer, will get its first taste of Taurus from June 19 to September 17. While the outer planets in Fire and Air signs will enjoy many harmonious interactions with each other, Chiron, the only significant slow-moving body in an Earth sign, will offer a dissonant note, poking holes in grandiose ideas that have lost touch with physical reality.

During Chiron's transit through individualistic Aries, which began in 2018, protest movements focused on racial or sexual identity labels have been prominent. When Chiron moves into money-focused Taurus, it's possible that the focus of collective feelings of woundedness will turn toward economic concerns.

ARIES

Your passion may be hard to miss this year, Aries. Say what you must, but try to keep an ear out for any feedback you receive.

SATURN AND NEPTUNE

You may be the face of the tension the collective is grappling with this year. Early in 2026, Saturn and Neptune both leave Pisces, your private 12th house, for your sign. Some big thoughts you've been chewing on internally for the past few years could therefore become public.

An idea that feels totally brilliant while you're pondering it alone might provoke an uncomfortable number of questions once you air it to others. However, try to avoid reacting in a defensive way. If you scare your critics off with a dramatic emotional display, they just might leave you alone to do your own thing — and allow you to discover for yourself whatever consequences they were going to warn you about!

With soggy Neptune in your sign, big feelings could be uncomfortably close to the surface. Neptune can blur past and present, making it easy for today's minor provocations to pull childhood wounds out of hiding. However, Saturn pushes you to pin down the progress that's physically possible here and now. You may have to abandon the hope of solving certain problems in order to free up your energy for the targets within your reach.

PLUTO

Manipulative Pluto will spend 2026 in your 11th House of Community, where it has already been off and on since 2023. This brings the possibility of subtle power dynamics in the friend groups and organizations you belong to. Control of information may be a prominent theme, whether you're involved in keeping a secret or frustrated that everyone else seems to know something you don't. Any conflict where you feel set apart from the crowd could peak on July 20, when Jupiter in your 5th House of Self-Expression opposes Pluto.

Pluto transiting your 11th house also gives you the potential to harness power and use it toward a good end, perhaps in the context of a political campaign or community organizing effort. Deep self-awareness is typically required to achieve the best-case scenario here. Think of your least favorite political viewpoint or party, and remember that the people who support it believe that they are doing the right thing just as sincerely as you believe that you are doing the right thing.

Even if it's totally true this time that you're right and your opponents are wrong, the victory you seek won't come without its costs. Achieving your preferred outcome could require you to do some things that challenge your ideals. Let whatever you learn from an encounter with your dark side soften your judgmental streak.

URANUS

In 2026, disruptive Uranus finishes its transit through Taurus, your 2nd House of Money. Any wild swings that you've experienced with your financial fortunes over the past several years are likely to calm down. If you've grown accustomed to being able to pull money out of your hat, that may no longer be possible. Your finances should become more predictable, for better or for worse.

Uranus then moves on to Gemini, your 3rd House of Communication, on April 25. You might become more comfortable taking risks in what you say to people. Try to think clearly about whether a risky statement you're considering is genuinely likely to bring a reward that's worth the trouble, though — don't just stir the pot for the sake of stirring the pot.

JUPITER

Abundant Jupiter begins the year in Cancer, which is your 4th House of Home and Family. Continuing the vibe of the second half of 2025, you may find it easier than usual to cultivate a domestic environment that is comfortable and nourishing.

Jupiter then moves into Leo, your 5th house, on June 29. This can bring you expansion in matters associated with children and creativity. If you want to get pregnant, it's potentially great; if you don't want to get pregnant, be careful.

The 5th house can also involve speculative and risky ways of making money. Perhaps you'll enjoy gains from something like cryptocurrency trading during the year that Jupiter is in Leo, but don't expect the boost to last forever!

CHIRON

Sorrowful Chiron has been in your sign since 2018, potentially drawing your attention toward ways you have been victimized throughout your life for your identity or physical characteristics. That particular weight may lift as Chiron moves on into Taurus, your money sector. You might then become acutely aware of negative contributions others have made to your present financial circumstances. However, you've probably learned quite a bit from the consequences of your own decisions over time too — consider how you can put that knowledge to use.

TAURUS

Feeling out of control is possible this year, Taurus. However, the part of any equation that you are most equipped to influence is what you bring to it, so looking within can be an excellent use of 2026's energies.

SATURN AND NEPTUNE

Early this year, strict Saturn and spacey Neptune will both leave your 11th House of Community for your contemplative 12th house. Perhaps it has been easy to blame society or the people around you for any restrictions or mixed messages that have made your life difficult lately.

However, the Saturn-Neptune conjunction in your 12th House of Self-Undoing on February 20 will turn your attention toward your own internal dynamics. You may actually find yourself separated from other people at this time. Whether or not it happens under circumstances of your choosing, a period of isolation can be good for you if you use it wisely.

It's okay to spend some of your downtime playing video games and pursuing other mindless fun. Your mind might be chewing on more complicated topics in the background. Still, try to put your insights into words once in a while, perhaps in a private journal.

PLUTO

In 2026, domineering Pluto will continue its transit of your 10th House of Authority. It might be easy for you to feel like others are picking on you and pushing you around. Sometimes this is true. Sometimes the truth is more complicated.

It's common for people to put out unconscious signals that contradict what they say and perhaps even sincerely believe that they want. These emanations are the domain of shadowy Pluto. You're currently especially likely to get caught up in a situation that involves mixed messages of this sort, whether you're dishing them out or receiving them.

Jupiter's opposition to Pluto on July 20 could be a fruitful time to begin unsnarling the confusion. At that time, abundant Jupiter will be in your 4th House of Foundations, increasing your sense of emotional security. When you feel basically good about yourself, taking dramatic actions to manipulate others into seeing you in a specific way may seem less appealing. Notice what you shed then.

URANUS

Your run as the weirdest person in the room is coming to an end. As unusual Uranus finishes its stay in your sign, you might reflect on how you've developed since 2018 in terms of your willingness to be different and stand out from the crowd. You probably had some big things that needed to be said. With that off your chest, though, now you'll have more space to listen to others share their experiences.

Uranus will then move on to Gemini, your 2nd House of Resources. Money matters could become more complex than you're used to them being. Perhaps you don't have to get all your income from the same source — a side gig or second job might provide a needed boost. However, it's possible for the level of activity to become overwhelming, so try to avoid getting spread too thin.

JUPITER

Jupiter begins 2026 in Cancer, your 3rd House of Communication. The level of chatter you experience with the people around you could be deafening, perhaps to the point you find it difficult to hear your own thoughts. Journaling can help you find the important information hidden in the noise.

Expansive Jupiter then moves into Leo, your domestic 4th house, on June 29. Changes involving your home or family are possible under this influence. Sometimes the changes will be immediately and obviously positive. In other cases, you might need to lose something you currently have in order to make room for new circumstances that will ultimately be more fulfilling. You don't need to pretend that such a loss doesn't hurt in the moment, especially if it wasn't your idea, but try to keep in mind the possibility of a bigger picture.

CHIRON

As melancholy Chiron explores your sign this summer, you might tend to feel sorry for yourself. The significations of the first house include your physical body, so any physical impairment that you experience has the potential to get pulled into a grand narrative of your overall victimization. It's not wrong to look for meaning and purpose in upsetting events, but try to stay aware of where your actual current somatic symptoms end and your story about them begins.

GEMINI

Your desire for intellectual connection could drive you to find your people in 2026. This quest has the potential to result in meaningful experiences, but maintaining a grounded perspective might be the hard part!

SATURN AND NEPTUNE

Your sense that the people in power have it in for you could be hard to shake. With repressive Saturn and fluctuating Neptune moving through your 10th House of Authority over the past several years, you've potentially felt jerked around by the whims of some oppressive figure.

Once Saturn and Neptune shift into your 11th House of Community in early 2026, you might be in the mood to rally a group to fight against whoever you have decided is keeping you down. Visionary Neptune brings idealism to this task — and also probably expectations that no human can possibly fill.

Gloomy Saturn in your 11th house could draw your attention toward the flaws of your social network. Meeting new people isn't a bad idea if you feel like you're not getting what you need from your current circle, but remember that you will bring yourself to the equation no matter where you go.

PLUTO

Pushy Pluto will continue its transit of your dogmatic 9th house throughout 2026. You may believe it is vitally important to convince the whole world to agree with you on some issue. Jupiter's opposition to Pluto on July 20 could coincide with a peak in your efforts to communicate your views.

Pluto can hide things from you, though. Although you may find it easy to scrutinize the motives of everyone around you, you'd likely benefit from turning that critical eye inward as well. Your intellectual journey over the past few years probably hasn't been a simple or straightforward one. Reflecting on how you've had to change, as well as acknowledging the dots you haven't been able to connect yet, could increase your empathy for others who don't seem to "get it" yet.

Pluto loves secrets and mysteries, so you might enjoy digging for information that is forbidden or not widely known while Pluto transits your 9th House of Higher Learning. Here's a big thought: if everyone else knew the most fascinating secret that you're currently obsessed with, would you still be interested in it?

URANUS

Innovative Uranus has been in your 12th House of the Subconscious since 2018, fomenting change behind the scenes. Now, as Uranus moves into your sign effective April 25, you'll likely be ready to start sharing some of the insights you've been chewing on in private.

As Uranus in your sign will trine Pluto in your philosophical 9th house, your political or spiritual beliefs might become a more prominent part of your identity than they have been in the past. This may bring you a level of intellectual fulfillment that you haven't had before, because signaling what you're into will help you find others who want the same things. However, relationships that have required you to hide or downplay your true desires are likely to struggle. Uranus demands individuality, often to the point of discomfort.

JUPITER

Abundant Jupiter begins 2026 in your 2nd House of

Resources. Continuing the theme of the second half of 2025, you might feel like money matters come more easily to you than usual. Take the opportunity to pay down debt and get necessary repairs done, as this influence won't last forever.

Jupiter then enters Leo, your 3rd House of Communication, on June 29. The natural flamboyance of your communication style is likely to be enhanced. You might as well have some fun with it, but make sure it stays fun — don't stir up potentially hurtful drama just to entertain yourself.

CHIRON

Any sense of social awkwardness you've been experiencing over the past several years might begin to lift as angsty Chiron starts making its way out of your 11th House of Community. Perhaps the people around you actually seem to like you at this point!

When Chiron pokes into your 12th House of Secrets, however, you might start to wonder if others would still like you if they knew certain information that you don't usually share. The bigger issue is probably whether you can like yourself in spite of that information. Start working there, and the rest of the picture should become less intimidating.

CANCER

Tender emotions could call for privacy this year, Cancer. You'll potentially have the opportunity to pursue a goal that matters to you, but haste makes waste — take the time you need to think everything through.

SATURN AND NEPTUNE

The Saturn-Neptune conjunction on February 20 will take place in your 10th House of Career, putting the dreams of Neptune in contact with the practical nature of Saturn. A grand vision may need to be pruned into a narrower form in order to be workable. If you're willing to sacrifice a few favorite parts of your fantasy, however, you'll probably have a chance to make quantifiable progress toward an outcome you find personally meaningful.

The 10th house also has to do with authority and power dynamics, so getting jerked around is possible with Saturn and Neptune in your 10th house. As Neptune is associated with suffering and attempts to relieve suffering, Neptune transiting your 10th house could bring about a situation where you feel compelled to go to great lengths to relieve someone else's suffering. Saturn wants clear rules to follow, but Neptune is unlikely to provide them. If nothing you do ever seems to make things right for the person you're helping, admitting that might ultimately help both of you choose more productive next steps.

Alternately, you might be the one who's seeking to wield power. There are situations where claiming a position of authority is completely appropriate, but you need to be totally realistic about what those situations are and are not. If you suspect that asking openly for what you want would result in a negative response, that's probably a sign you're on the wrong track.

PLUTO

During 2026, shadowy Pluto will continue its transit through your 8th House of Shared Resources. The rules, spoken or unspoken, that govern your connection with another person or institution could seem to be full of traps that only ever seem to catch you.

Still, even if it's true that a person or circumstance you're entangled with is holding you back, that's not necessarily the whole story. As brilliant Uranus in your 12th House of Confinement works collaboratively with

Pluto, perhaps being blocked from certain possibilities gives you more time and energy to focus on your intellectual life.

Jupiter's opposition to Pluto on July 20 could bring a plot twist. Perhaps you've long been the more vulnerable party in the exchange. However, with abundant Jupiter in your personal finance zone, you might suddenly be better equipped to take care of yourself. Watching how the dynamic then shifts will likely be informative.

URANUS

Energetic Uranus has been in your 11th House of Social Networking since 2018. This probably brought a lot of interesting people into your life. However, it potentially also provided opportunities to get swept up in exciting group activities before you had a chance to decide what was really the right fit for you personally.

Once Uranus shifts into your 12th House of Contemplation on April 25, you'll likely have a transformative amount of alone time. It's okay if you don't share a new subject of interest with others as soon as you discover it. Leave the risk of their judgment out of the equation as long as you need to.

JUPITER

Fortunate Jupiter begins 2026 in your sign, where it spent the second half of 2025. This can increase your confidence, and your positive attitude in turn can bring positive outcomes on a variety of subjects. You might also see yourself as generous toward others with money or helpful advice; keep a realistic eye on how your efforts of this sort land before you take them too far.

Jupiter then shifts into Leo, your 2nd House of Resources, on June 29. An increase in the amount of money available to you is possible at this time. However, it isn't guaranteed to last beyond the year that Jupiter stays in Leo, so use any bonus to pay down debts and take care of needed repairs while you have the chance.

CHIRON

As touchy Chiron moves into your 11th House of Social Networking this summer, you may tend to see the worst in your peers' interactions with you. If you're worried that others will judge you harshly for some aspect of your personal life, limiting what you share with them is a step you can take for your own comfort.

You might also find it helpful to join a support group geared toward a particular problem that is weighing on you. Conversations where everyone shares that basic common ground are likely to feel easier than conversations where you have to explain your whole situation from scratch.

LEO

The glare of the spotlight could get intense during the second half of 2026, Leo. For better or for worse, you're likely to get noticed in a way you haven't been in a while!

SATURN AND NEPTUNE

Refining your personal philosophy is possible this year. On February 20, Saturn and Neptune will conjoin in your 9th House of Travel and Higher Learning. The 9th house has to do with your beliefs about the world, including your political and spiritual views.

Neptune adds idealism and emotionalism to any viewpoint, while Saturn demands logic and structure. If your argument manages to satisfy both Saturnian and Neptunian longings, you're likely on the right track!

However, it's easy to become discouraged while taking on such a demanding task. You might therefore come to idealize some other culture that appears to have everything figured out. Learn what you can from any teacher who resonates with you, but remember that every locale has its problems.

PLUTO

Relationship drama could seem impossible to untangle as intimidating Pluto continues its transit through your 7th House of Partnerships. Perhaps you and another person are both too afraid to talk to each other.

Pushing through your fear no matter what isn't always the best option. Sometimes it's wise to avoid asking questions you don't want answered.

However, you are within your rights to follow what flows more naturally at this time. You may never get the closure you crave in a connection that's stuck at a painful impasse. If you prioritize other relationships that are just easier to deal with, though, your unresolvable wound may get the space it needs to gradually lose its charge.

URANUS

Your professional life is about to calm down. Revolutionary Uranus has been in your 10th House of Career since 2018, encouraging you to prioritize bold moves over predictability and stability. Some of those shifts likely improved your overall status and prospects, but the process was probably also nerve-racking! Fortunately, you're at a point where you can start to take what you've learned and use it in a less chaotic way.

Once Uranus moves into Gemini, your 11th House of Community, your social life could become more stressful, at least temporarily. Perhaps you've managed to hide your wilder side from some of your friends and acquaintances. That polite subterfuge is likely to blow open. Disclosure won't necessarily be the end of the world, though — maybe it'll inspire others to air secrets of their own.

JUPITER

Indulgent Jupiter spends the first half of 2026 in Cancer, your 12th House of Contemplation. You'll potentially find this time boring, as not a lot is necessarily happening in the outside world for you. However, you need the rest to prepare for what's to come.

On June 29, Jupiter will enter your sign, drawing attention your way. You're likely to take up more space. Sometimes this is even literal to the point of physically gaining weight. Your increased visibility could inspire others to offer you rewarding opportunities. However, you're going to be conspicuous no matter what you're up to, so make sure you're not doing anything bad!

CHIRON

Suffering could become part of your public image as wounded Chiron spends this summer in your 10th House of Reputation. The story of a tragic event in your life, whether recent or long ago, may suddenly be aired. Maybe it'll be a relief for you to have others finally understand a key part of why you are the way you are. Even so, being visible for this sort of thing isn't always fun. Noting how you've learned and grown from the experience can make the tale less depressing for both you and your audience.

VIRGO

You're probably more ready than you think you are for a big shift in your public role. Although feelings of vulnerability are probably an unavoidable part of such a transition, the good news for you is that change also has a manageable practical side!

SATURN AND NEPTUNE

The Saturn-Neptune conjunction on February 20 takes place in your 8th House of Shared Resources. With the structuring influence of Saturn in play, you have a chance to set up an arrangement for sharing money or property that actually works. However, doing so will probably require you to abandon certain Neptunian dreams about how such arrangements *should* work.

Regarding the Neptune component, you will likely have to confront a long-held desire to be taken care of. You may know that you *shouldn't* want something like that, which probably only makes you want it more.

It's possible to acknowledge your longings without shaming them. What is workable in practice may still be different, but that's another conversation.

PLUTO

Intense Pluto continues its sojourn through your 6th House of Daily Routines this year. At baseline, your sign has a reputation for nitpicking. This transit could really dial that up!

Jupiter's opposition to Pluto on July 20 is a good opportunity for you to get perspective on your worries. Although your radar sometimes picks up valid problems, especially in the realm of health and wellness, hyperfocus there can also be used to compensate for uncertainty about the bigger things in life. With nourishing Jupiter in your 12th House of Contemplation at that time, you may find it easier than usual to tolerate not knowing all the answers.

Meanwhile, your attention to detail might find a constructive outlet in your professional life. As revolutionary Uranus in your 10th House of Career trines Pluto, having the basics nailed down can provide the foundation you need to successfully pull off a bold move.

URANUS

Quirky Uranus has been in your 9th House of Beliefs since 2018, encouraging you to follow your curiosity and embrace perspectives that aren't necessarily popular. Perhaps it's been a little challenging to tell the difference between an idea you just find interesting and one you want to seriously commit to.

As Uranus shifts into your goal-oriented 10th house on April 25, you'll likely find it easier to discern which viewpoints you're ready to pursue further. This might ultimately involve taking a stand that doesn't make everybody happy. However, some will probably appreciate your leadership, so try to direct your attention there.

JUPITER

Enthusiastic Jupiter begins 2026 in your 11th House of Community, keeping your social calendar busy. You're likely to have a prominent role in at least one organization or friend group, perhaps to the point that you feel overwhelmed by all the activity.

The rest you crave could come in the second half of the year, after Jupiter moves into your contemplative 12th house on June 29. At that point, you'll have an opportunity to enjoy your rich inner life. Fantasizing isn't necessarily a waste of time — perhaps portions of a good daydream will manifest in a workable plan down the road!

CHIRON

In summer 2026, defensive Chiron will explore your philosophical 9th house, perhaps heightening your sensitivity to slights against your spiritual or political beliefs. It's possible that you genuinely could be mistreated by others for reasons of that sort. That said, no matter how out of line your opponents are, not everything that goes wrong is necessarily their fault. Keep a close eye on how well the claims you espouse are working out *for you*.

LIBRA

Is it ever *not* about relationship drama for you, Libra? Your ongoing quest to find balance between self and other is likely to command a lot of your attention in 2026. For once, however, it has the potential to be a fair fight.

SATURN AND NEPTUNE

Your patience for flakiness is likely to fade this year. As decisive Saturn shifts into your 7th House of Partnerships, you may be eager to pin down answers regarding where you stand with the significant people in your life. Unfortunately, foggy Neptune, also entering your 7th house, might prevent you from achieving the clarity you crave.

Sometimes the mixed message *is* the message. If a person you consider important isn't willing to talk frankly with you, they might not be as invested in the connection as you are. Alternately, they may simply be in a chaotic place for reasons that aren't really about you. Be realistic about the limitations of such individuals, and look elsewhere if they can't give you what you need.

At best, the combination of structured Saturn and idealistic Neptune in your 7th house has the potential to bring you a committed relationship where shared spiritual views are a big part of your connection. This might refer to a romance, a serious friendship, a business partnership, or receiving care from some sort of healer. Do what you can to make your vision manifest, but also stay open to the possibility of events unfolding in a way better than anything you could have planned!

PLUTO

Throughout 2026, powerful Pluto continues its transit of your 5th House of Self-Expression. The opportunity to prioritize your own desires might still feel like an unfamiliar experience for you. You're coming down from Pluto's transit through your domestic 4th house, which spanned from 2008 to 2024 and potentially put you on the receiving end of heavy demands from family members.

The hard part of your newfound freedom is potentially that no one is telling you what to do. As arrogant Jupiter in your social sector opposes Pluto on July 20, something your peers do could rub you the wrong way, thereby giving you useful intel regarding what you *don't* want.

On the other hand, seeing someone else embark on a bold journey might give you the idea that you're capable of poking outside your usual surroundings too. With a Saturn-ruled 4th house, you're potentially a bit of a homebody at baseline. However, as refreshing Uranus in your expansive 9th house aligns harmoniously with Pluto, travel might be especially fulfilling!

URANUS

Thinking realistically about what your independence has cost you might be necessary now. Since 2018, rebellious Uranus has been transiting your 8th House of Shared Resources, potentially fueling a sense that you need to be totally separate from others in order to have any freedom at all. Although this approach may have initially been necessary to get you out of an unfair situation, perhaps you're starting to discover its limits.

On April 25, Uranus shifts into your philosophical 9th house, which also governs rules and laws. You might be less averse to collaborating with others if you had reason to believe that doing so wouldn't just result in you getting exploited one more time. Making expectations clear from the beginning can help you start any new connections out on the right foot.

JUPITER

Helpful Jupiter begins 2026 in your 10th House of Purpose. The hard part of this, Libra, is that it has to do with finding *your* purpose, which might be different from the purpose that a family member has in mind for you, and maybe you're afraid that telling them no would hurt them too much. With nurturing Cancer for your 10th house, you probably feel a strong pull to take care of others who are in pain. You don't have to abandon that pursuit entirely, but look for a way to do it that will bring you the financial security you need.

On June 29, Jupiter moves into Leo, your 11th House of Community. This could at least bring relief from any family tensions awakened by Jupiter's transit through your 10th house, as you're likely to be reminded that the world is much bigger than your family. Have fun putting yourself out there and meeting all kinds of people!

CHIRON

In 2026, world-weary Chiron will begin to leave your 7th House of Relationships for your 8th House of Shared Resources. On both relevant subjects, you're potentially smarter than you get credit for being, even if you haven't met certain socially recognized milestones yet. You've likely learned some painful lessons about the things that can go wrong when you let others into your life, but try to recognize when you've integrated the lesson — something you needed to avoid for a period of time may not need to be avoided forever.

SCORPIO

Knowing your limits will be key in 2026, Scorpio. Other people likely need less of your focus than you're inclined to give them, so direct your energy toward making manageable improvements in your personal life instead.

SATURN AND NEPTUNE

Hypochondria has the potential to run amok this year. As the Saturn-Neptune conjunction takes place in your 6th House of Health and Wellness on February 20, a scary-sounding health concern might command your attention. Even if something is genuinely wrong, it may be hard to know where the actual problem ends and the catastrophizing about it begins.

After Saturn and Neptune complete their conjunction, elusive Neptune will continue hanging out in your 6th house until 2039, so there will probably be a lot that you can't know. Disciplined Saturn's transit through your 6th house will be shorter, only lasting until 2028, so it's a great opportunity to start habits that can carry you onward.

Any routine that's going to stick will have to realistically accept the limits of the things you can't know and the things you can't change. You may also have to acknowledge that your energy levels won't always be the same from day to day. Within those parameters, though, it's probably possible to have some of the freedom you crave!

PLUTO

Finding the right answer to family challenges could seem impossible as unconscious Pluto continues its journey through your 4th House of Home and Family. Your 4th house, Aquarius, actually has two rulers — repressive Saturn and rebellious Uranus. Perhaps you're dealing with someone who wants to have it both ways and can therefore never be pleased. Alternately, maybe you're the one with contradictory expectations.

As unconventional Uranus trines Pluto throughout the second half of the year, embracing the Uranian side of your 4th house might be your most realistic path toward positive change. The less you try to make your family life measure up to the standard, real or imagined, of what other families are doing, the better.

It's also highly likely that each person in the equation needs more space than they presently have to do their own thing. Although it might be tempting for you to dream up a grand solution that would fix every conceivable problem for everyone, try to keep your focus on what you can personally do to make yourself more comfortable here and now.

URANUS

With volatile Uranus in your 7th House of Relationships, perhaps some of the significant people in your life have seemed unpredictable and harsh over the past several years. Well, *of course* they've been unpredictable — unfortunately, Scorpio, they're separate human beings whose decisions aren't yours to predict or control!

Wanting to know what to expect doesn't make you a monster, but you need to find a way to achieve this outcome without suffocating your loved ones. As independent Uranus settles in your 8th House of Shared Resources on April 25, what might help you most is taking a big step back from everyone else. Figure out processes that keep your life flowing whether or not others choose to join you, and that could eventually give them enough room to wander over on their own terms.

JUPITER

Confident Jupiter begins 2026 in your 9th House of Beliefs, where it also spent the second half of 2025. With emotive Cancer for your 9th house, you're likely to be passionate about your political and spiritual views at baseline, and adding a Jupiter transit into the mix could really dial that up.

At some point, however, being right might require more than scaring others into silence with a big emotional display. After Jupiter moves into Leo, your 10th House of Fame and Reputation, on June 29, you could wind up with a more public position than you usually have — whether you asked for this change or not! Any inconsistencies in your story may then become apparent under the glare of the spotlight, so try to muster the humility to start cleaning things up now.

CHIRON

Your relationships could start to take on a different sort of intensity this summer. Although your sign has a reputation for loving drama and intrigue, what sensitive Chiron has to offer is less sensational. Instead of having clear heroes and villains, you might wind up with the sort of situation where everyone is obviously doing their best and the outcome is still painful. With blame less of an option than usual, you might finally have to experience the more vulnerable feelings that blame typically protects you from.

SAGITTARIUS

Drowning in the past is a risk for you this year, Sagittarius. If you're willing to accept the challenge of learning a few new things, you might find that living in the present has its perks!

SATURN AND NEPTUNE

I'm going to switch gears and tell you a story. I recently paid $11.11 for access to a guided meditation I heard about on Instagram that was supposed to help me get past common blocks to financial abundance. I started listening to the recording and was directed to take myself back to an upsetting childhood experience. After the speaker explored that scene for a while, she then asked me to change the scene so that it went the way I wanted it to go differently.

I stopped listening to the recording because I didn't know how I wanted that scene to go differently. The scene had to do with dynamics surrounding a family member's medical condition in my early childhood.[2] It's probably fair to say that the situation was traumatic

---

[2] The person with the medical condition in this case was actually *not* my dad, whose medical issues I wrote about in *Changing of the Guards: Pluto on the Precipice.*

for everyone involved. However, I can't quite simply wish that the medical condition had never existed because I also see how the efforts to find relief for the person who was suffering ultimately got the whole household eating a healthier diet than it otherwise might have — and we'll never know whether being pushed to make that change protected us from experiencing an even worse outcome.

As gloomy Saturn and sentimental Neptune meet in your 5th House of Children on February 20, you too may be inspired to reflect on upsetting scenes from your childhood. Alternately, you might be disappointed with the way your children have turned out, or the consequences of a past decision to have or not have children could be weighing on you.

Whatever the issue is, ask yourself how you wanted things to go differently. If it turns out that you can't get rid of the part of the story you don't want without also getting rid of good things that came from the painful experience, that might provide the perspective you need.

PLUTO

In 2026, subversive Pluto will continue its journey through your 3rd House of Communication. Your words could be more powerful than you think they are, so it's possible for you to hurt people without really meaning to. You're chewing on intense topics, and your efforts to satisfy your curiosity may come off as intrusive or creepy to others who simply aren't on that wavelength at this time.

As liberating Uranus in your relationship zone trines Pluto throughout the second half of the year, however, you might have opportunities to find others who are up for the same challenges you are. These are likely to be people who are new to you rather than people you've known for most of your life. Although you may really want to convince your longtime posse of the correctness of your approach, trying to push through their resistance just takes away from the time you could spend pursuing connections that flow more naturally.

URANUS

At baseline, you might tend to live in your head rather than your body. With disruptive Uranus in your 6th House of Daily Routines since 2018, however, the physical world has probably made its presence impossible to ignore.

Starting April 25, Uranus will commit to staying in Gemini, your 7th House of Relationships. This might be easier for you in some ways, as it has the potential to provide the sort of intellectual connection you enjoy. Then again, sometimes getting what you think you want isn't so easy! It won't be all about you pontificating and showing off how smart you are — your companions are going to insist on having their say too.

JUPITER

Jupiter, your sign's ruler, will be in Cancer, your 8th House of Shared Resources for the first half of 2026. This could actually be good for you financially. Perhaps you'll finally receive the support you need from someone else to make a significant step toward a goal of yours.

Once extravagant Jupiter gets involved, though, knowing when to stop is often the hard part. After Jupiter moves into Leo, your 9th House of Beliefs, on June 29, you could be tempted to make a big show of how right you are about some issue, especially if it involves politics or religion. Jupiter's opposition to Pluto on July 20 might bring up a lesson that was in a *Bluey* book I got for my niece — sometimes you have to choose between being right and being able to keep playing together.

CHIRON

Moody Chiron has been in your individualistic 5th house since 2018, heightening your awareness of your inner child's wounds. Perhaps you've sometimes felt like no one else had it as rough as you did growing up — the 5th house can be self-centered in that way.

This summer, Chiron will begin moving into your 6th House of Health and Wellness. Although you might be distressed by physical complaints you experience at this time, the upside is that you'll potentially find present-day physical answers for them. Having this sort of tangible problem could seem easier than battling against the ghosts of the past. Feel free to take pride in your ability to learn new information!

CAPRICORN

Security could be a sore spot for you in 2026, Capricorn. There will probably be some amount of chaos no matter what you do, but embracing your own weird side might actually tip the energetic scales in your favor!

SATURN AND NEPTUNE

Finding a comfortable container could be challenging at present. With dreamy Neptune moving into your 4th House of Home, you may like the idea of a living situation that has less structure than you're used to. However, disciplined Saturn is also entering your 4th house at roughly the same time, and it wants to know what to expect.

Keeping things simple might be key to keeping them flexible. Lightening your load of material possessions can make it easier for you to change your residence if you need to. That said, remember that the grass isn't always greener somewhere else. Be realistic about whether moving is equipped to solve the problem you want it to solve before you go to all the trouble of actually doing it.

Wherever you wind up, you're likely to be sensitive to the spiritual and energetic dimensions of your surroundings. Taking up feng shui or a similar discipline could help you translate vibes into practical action.

PLUTO

Money matters may not follow a straightforward path for you at this time. As mysterious Pluto continues passing through your 2nd House of Resources, perhaps the effort you invest doesn't quite match the rewards you reap.

Your unspoken expectations might be a crucial missing piece of the equation. If you truly want to solve a money problem, looking at the actual flow of money in and out of your account should give you some answers. If obtaining emotional security is a more compelling priority for you, that's not necessarily wrong, but admit it, and admit that that's what you're spending your money on.

As experimental Uranus in your 6th House of Work trines Pluto throughout the second half of 2026, accepting a job that's a little chaotic for the time being could serve as an important financial or professional stepping stone. That said, keep an eye on when you've learned what you need to learn from the experience; don't let your sense of loyalty keep you chained to someone else's drama indefinitely.

URANUS

Uninhibited Uranus has been in your pleasure-oriented 5th house since 2018, drawing your attention toward what feels good for you. That said, perhaps you've been able to keep your hedonistic side compartmentalized to some extent. Your sign has a reputation for preferring a serious, buttoned-up image, and there are probably settings where you still maintain that.

As Uranus settles in your 6th House of Daily Routines starting April 25, your ability to compartmentalize may fade. Your more interesting interests could become a more obvious part of your life than they currently are. Although that visibility won't always be comfortable, consider the alternative. Uranus is going to bring the weirdness, whether it's your weirdness or the weirdness of someone else you get involved with, so it might as well be your weirdness!

JUPITER

As fortunate Jupiter begins 2026 in your 7th House of Partnerships, starting a rewarding new relationship is possible. However, sometimes you have to get there from here first. Jupiter expands, so it might expand you out of an established relationship that doesn't give you enough room to grow.

Jupiter's next stop after that is your 8th House of Shared Resources, starting June 29. It's possible that you'll become closely connected with someone who has more wealth or status than you do. Especially as Jupiter opposes manipulative Pluto on July 20, beware of offers that come with too many strings attached.

CHIRON

Angsty Chiron has been transiting your 4th House of Roots since 2018, perhaps stirring up hard feelings about your family or your upbringing. This summer, Chiron will poke into your 5th House of Pleasure, potentially offering insight regarding your approach to romance or other fun pursuits. You could come to realize that there's often an element of overcompensating for something else when you indulge yourself. The underlying problem may or may not be fixable, but try to at least be aware of the dynamic.

AQUARIUS

Your voice is likely to be powerful in 2026, Aquarius. As long as you stay tethered to the truth, you have a strong chance of delivering a message that makes an impact.

SATURN AND NEPTUNE

Being careful with your words could be crucial now. As slippery Neptune slides into your 3rd House of Communication, you may find it easy to see how putting a certain spin on things makes it more likely that you'll get what you want. Unfortunately, Saturn, the planet of consequences, is also entering your 3rd house, increasing the chances that you'll get called out for any inconsistencies in your story.

How do you thread this needle? If you have a true statement to make about a genuine problem, you might as well make it. Neptune will give you support to do so in a way that touches the emotions of your audience.

However, you don't want your audience to wind up emotionally overwhelmed to the point of paralysis. Logical Saturn can help you rein in the more triggering parts of your tale and keep the focus on practical steps that you and others can take to address the problem.

PLUTO

Staying out of trouble could be a struggle these days. With polarizing Pluto in your sign, other people could easily get the idea that any disturbance on their radar came from you on purpose. Perhaps you intended nothing of the sort, but you might actually start to believe that you're at fault if you get blamed loudly and repeatedly enough for some awful deed.

Of course, when shadowy Pluto is in the mix, nothing is quite what it appears to be. What's potentially secretly seductive for you in accepting scapegoat status? If people think you're powerful enough to cause all their problems, they must think you're pretty darn powerful!

Direct confrontation is possible when cocky Jupiter in your relationship sector opposes Pluto on July 20. Otherwise, the tension might mostly simmer under the surface. Use any periods of relative quiet to determine what you'd do if you really were *that* powerful.

URANUS

Any domestic upheaval you've been experiencing could begin to ease. With volatile Uranus in your 4th House of Home and Family since 2018, maybe you've moved around from one residence to another because you just can't get comfortable. Alternately, perhaps you've stayed in the same place but kept it chaotic with constant compulsive remodeling projects.

With Uranus settling in your 5th House of Self-Expression on April 25, you might be able to express yourself more straightforwardly. Especially as Uranus trines Pluto throughout the second half of 2026, you'll likely have support to air deep frustrations that are weighing on you. Perhaps your grievance is something that others really need to hear!

JUPITER

Optimistic Jupiter will begin 2026 in your 6th House of Health and Wellness, perhaps providing the boost you need to get out of a rut. Once you're feeling good physically, it may then be easy to take on one too many things, so try to stay realistic about your bandwidth.

On June 29, Jupiter will migrate into your 7th House of Relationships. Meeting someone helpful to you is possible under this influence. However, there could be an uneven power dynamic between the two of you. If you're intentionally seeking out a teacher or counselor, that's an expected part of the arrangement. Speak up instead of seething if you feel like you're getting bossed around in an inappropriate way, though.

CHIRON

This summer, Chiron will enter your 4th House of Roots, turning your attention toward difficult family dynamics. Something about your current home or family situation might trigger memories of what you needed and didn't get growing up. Although you probably have more freedom to handle things differently now, doing so may not immediately resolve your emotional wounds about the past — allow that to be its own process.

PISCES

It's not all about you, Pisces, and that's a good thing! Your lessons in 2026 are likely to include learning to relate to others in a more balanced way.

SATURN AND NEPTUNE

The pressure on you to be everything to everyone might finally dissipate. Compassionate Neptune has been in your sign since 2011, and practical Saturn has been there since 2023. Although you may have initially celebrated when the Neptune in Pisces transit made it cool to be sensitive, perhaps it eventually became overwhelming — even you have limits!

Once Saturn and Neptune settle in Aries in early 2026, you may wind up with a less prominent role in the collective, giving you room to restore your energy and reflect on the bigger picture. Saturn and Neptune will then be in your 2nd House of Resources, and that's likely to narrow your focus in a good way. If you're asked whether or not you *care* about a particular cause, how could you say no? If you have a finite amount of money to distribute, however, you'll probably have to make some decisions about what's most deserving of your support.

That said, you'll also have to take care to see your pot of money accurately. Although Saturn prides itself on being logical and precise, it also has a pessimistic streak that can make things look worse than they really are. Meanwhile, Neptune loves the opportunity to tell a dramatic story. Even if it's true that you don't currently have all the resources you'd like to have, avoid spinning that into a narrative of Dickensian poverty — give yourself room to grow.

PLUTO

Throughout 2026, mysterious Pluto will remain in your 12th House of Self-Undoing, perhaps making it obvious that your negative habits are holding you back. That said, shaming yourself won't help. Keep in mind that any destructive pattern you can't seem to shake was probably adopted for a reason — perhaps it protected you from a valid threat you faced at an earlier time in your life.

As refreshing Uranus in your 4th House of Roots trines Pluto throughout the second half of 2026, you'll have a unique opportunity to look at your formative experiences in a new way. Although your past will still be whatever it was, you may be able to change how you relate to it in the present. Try to take pride in the lessons you've learned instead of lamenting the amount of time you wasted in unpleasant circumstances.

With stubborn Pluto parked in your 12th house until 2044, you may continue to be stuck in circumstances that don't seem to be of your choosing for a while. Whatever the whole story might be there, external markers of wealth and status aren't the only part of it worth considering — if your current activities are making you think, that's a productive use of your time!

URANUS

Wacky Uranus has been stimulating your 3rd House of Communication since 2018, and perhaps you've grown to enjoy causing a stir by making shocking comments. You've potentially put forth some genuinely good ideas in the course of all this, but maybe you've also said a few things you don't actually believe just to get a reaction from your audience.

This desire for attention could be coming from a sense of insecurity. After independent Uranus shifts into your 4th House of Foundations on April 25, you might become less interested in what others think of you. It's not always wrong to rock the boat, but you'll have a better sense of when that truly needs doing once your craving for validation is no longer running the show.

JUPITER

For the first half of 2026, upbeat Jupiter will be in your playful 5th house, putting you in touch with your creative side. This enhanced ability to find fun in life could take the edge off some of the more challenging transits you have at this time.

On June 29, Jupiter will move into your responsible 6th house, giving you a lift in matters of health as well as work. However, you may wind up busier than you really find comfortable, especially if a job or volunteer opportunity is presented in a way that flatters your ego. You might as well build up your resume while you have the chance, but keep an eye on your energy level.

CHIRON

Anxious Chiron has been in your money sector since 2018, perhaps fueling a desire to send a message to others by accumulating wealth or material possessions. You'll potentially find out whether anyone has even been paying attention when Chiron peeks into your 3rd House of Communication this summer. Although you may fear that having direct conversations about the issues that weigh on you will result in your feelings getting hurt, too much implying and assuming can create real problems. Keep in mind that there are possibilities worse than occasionally being told things you don't want to hear.

ABOUT THE AUTHOR

Eva Sylwester began exploring astrology and other new frontiers in spirituality shortly after she earned her BA in psychology and religious studies from the University of Oregon in 2007. She has written horoscopes for Tarot.com and curates Weekend Entertainment Guide on her Substack. She is a lifelong resident of Eugene, Oregon.

astrologybooks.substack.com

www.amazon.com/author/evasylwester